INSURANCE WHAT YOU DON'T KNOW

BY PATRICK U UMEH

Copyright © 2014 by Patrick U Umeh

Insurance what you don't know
by Patrick U Umeh

Printed in the United States of America

ISBN 9781498404488

All rights reserved solely by the author. The author guarantees all contents are original and do not infringe upon the legal rights of any other person or work. No part of this book may be reproduced or transmitted In any form or in any means, electronic, or mechanical, Including photocopying and recording or by information Storage or retrieval system without prior written and expressed permission of the author. The views expressed in this book are not necessarily those of the publisher.

Scripture quotations taken from the New International Version (NIV). Copyright © 1973, 1978, 1984, 2011 by Biblica, Inc.™. Used by permission. All rights reserved.

www.xulonpress.com

CONTENTS

CHAPTER 1 Early Development of Insurance 15

CHAPTER 2 General Concept of Insurance 20

CHAPTER 3 The Miracle of Life Insurance 34

CHAPTER 4 Payment of Claims...43

CHAPTER 5 OBAMA CARE 51

CHAPTER 6 Articles and References.................................57

ACKNOWLEDGMENTS

First and foremost, I thank God for making this book a reality.
Great thanks to my wife, Mrs. Ugonma Jessica Umeh for her encouragements and unflinching support.

Special thanks to my parents Emmanuel and Hannah Umeh. Through their words and examples, I quickly learned that whatever I vividly imagined, ardently desired, and enthusiastically acted upon, must unavoidably come to pass. They are simply, "the winds beneath my wings."

Thanks also to my Clients, the United States Postal Services, Humana Health Care Plans, Inc., Blue Cross and Blue shield of Kentucky Inc., Continental General Life, National Foundation Life, Life U.S.A. A.L. Hansel Paint Inc., Walter Cabinets Inc., to mention just a few.

Your contracts with our company provided a real practical experience, thus enabling us to "practice what we preach."

Dedicated to my Children.

PREFACE

This book is written to answer the most commonly asked questions about insurance.

Students aspiring to pursue a career in insurance or related fields will find this book very informative, as it is based on over 25 years of practical experience in the Financial Service Industry.

Similarly, the uniqueness of this book can be well explained in these worlds:

I came, I saw, I conquered. (Veni vidi vici)
Julius Caesar Letter to Amantius, 47 B.C.

I READ, I PRACTICED, I WROTE.
Patrick Umeh

"One of the greatest pieces of economic wisdom is to know what you do not know."

G.K. Galbraith

A Moment of Reflection

Three Religious Leaders

Three religious leaders, a Jewish Rabbi, a Catholic priest, and a Protestant Minister, respectively went fishing together in a small boat. The Rabbi, suddenly remembering he had left his fishing pole at the cabin, stepped out of the boat and walked on the water to the shore.

Just then, the Priest remarked that he had left his lure behind and he, too, stepped over the side of the boat and followed in the same direction as the Rabbi.

When they both returned to the boat, the Protestant Minister who had watched the remarkable demonstration reasoned, "Now, my faith must be as strong as theirs." Determinedly, he stepped out into the water and immediately sank to the bottom.

His two companions dragged him out, but once again he made a determined effort of faith, and again sank into the water. "My faith must be as strong as yours; why can't I walk on the water like you?" he asked his rescuers.

The Rabbi turned to the Priest and said, "We'd better tell him where those rocks are before he drowns himself."

"Field and trees teach me nothing, but the people in a city do."
                                                        Socrates

CHAPTER 1

EARLY DEVELOPMENT OF INSURANCE

Insurance is almost as old as the world in which we live. The so-called bottomry contracts were known to merchants of Babylon as early as 4000-3000 BC. Bottomry were practiced by the Hindus and the ancient Greeks as early as the 4th century BC. Under bottomry contract, loans were granted to merchants with the provision that if the shipment was lost at sea, the loan would not have to be repaid.

Ancient Roman law recognized the bottomry contract; to foster its administration, an article of agreement was drawn up, and funds were deposited with a money changer.

In West Africa, especially in the southeastern part of Nigeria, occupied by a tribe known as the IBO's, a form of insurance was noticed hundreds of years ago before the colonization of West Africa. This type of insurance was early known as Ogbo (group survival). The villagers of these groups entered into a pact with each other so as to withstand any external aggression and were bonded by a principle known as, "Enyi_mba_Enyi" (the strength or law of large numbers).

Hunting was the principal occupation of these communities, and they moved in groups to ensure the safety of individuals. When prey was killed, the meat had to be shared among all the members

> *"Reviewers are usually people who would have been poets, historians, Biographers , if they could: they have tried their talents at one or the other, and have failed; therefore they turn critics."*
>
> S.T. Coleridge

of the group, regardless of who actually captured and slew the prey.

This method of shared risk became the first form of risk-spreading, assuring equitable, fair, and just distribution of their resources.

There were no written contracts or policy guidelines to bind these groups; however, an oral contract known as ogburuke (let he who kills share) was strongly implemented. All members were required to abide by this principle.

Although the strength of ogburuke dwindled as the society grew complex, the peace of mind provided by this formal group to its members can never be overestimated.

In England, fire insurance arose much later, obtaining impetus from the Great Fire of London in 1966. A number of other insurance companies were started during the so-called Bubble Era in England after 1711. They were more or less fraudulent, mismanaged, and were prompted by the economic forces to fold up. Nevertheless, two important and successful English insurance companies were formed during this period–the London Assurance Corporation and the Royal Exchange Assurance Corporation. Their operations marked the beginning of modern property and the liability insurance.

Our discussion of the early development of insurance in Europe will never be complete without reference to the Lloyds of London, the International Insurance Market. It began in the 17th century as a coffee house patronized by merchants, bankers, and insurance underwriters, gradually becoming recognized as the most likely place to find underwriters for marine insurance. Edward Lloyd supplied his customers with shipping information gathered from the docks and other sources; this eventually grew into the publication Lloyd's List, still in existence.

"Fame is what you have taken, character is what you give; When to truth you waken; then you begin to live."
Baynard Taylor

Lloyd's was reorganized in 1769 as a formal group of underwriters accepting marine risks. (The word underwriter is said to be derived from the practice of having each risk taker write his name under total amounts of risk that he was willing to accept at a specified premium.) With the growth of British Sea power, Lloyd's became the dominant insurer of marine risks to which were later added fire and other property risks.

In the United States, the first insurance company was organized by Benjamin Franklin in 1752 as the Philadelphia Contributionship. The first life insurance company in the American colonies was the Presbyterian Minister Fund, organized in 1759. By 1820, there were 17 stock life insurance companies in the state of New York alone. Many of the early property insurance companies failed from speculative investments, poor management, and inadequate distribution systems. Others failed after the Chicago fire in 1871 and San Francisco fire and earth quake of 1906. There was little effective regulation and rate making was difficult in the absence of cooperative development of sound statistics. Many problems also beset the life insurance business. In the era following the U.S. Civil War, bad practices developed; dividends were declared that had not been earned, reserves were inadequate, advertising claims were exaggerated and office buildings were erected that sometimes cost more than the total assets of the companies. As a result, thirty-three life insurance companies failed between 1870 and 1872 and another 48 between 1873 and 1877.

After 1910, life insurance enjoyed a steady growth in the United States. The annual growth rate of insurance in force over the period 1910-82 was approximately 8.2 percent, amounting to a 300-fold increase in the 72-year period.

In 1982, nearly $4,500,000,000,000 of life insurance was in force. The assets of more than 2,000 U.S. life insurance companies totaled nearly $600,000,000,000, making life insurance one of the largest

"The wheel that squeaks the loudest is the one that gets the grease."
Josh Billings, The Kicker

savings institutions in the United States. Today with the advancement of modern medicine and increased standard of living, life expectancy is higher. As a result, life insurance companies are now experiencing their highest growth rate ever.

"No one can make you feel inferior without your consent."
Eleanor Roosevelt

A moment of Reflection
Positive Mental Attitude

Each morning when I wake up, I will awaken with a positive mental attitude. This attitude will be with me all the rest of the day. As I become aware of the negative people, who are constantly saying,

"You can't do that.
You don't know how.
You are going to fail,"
It stimulates me to become more positive.

Pat Umeh

"The fountains mingle with the river,
And the rivers with the ocean;
The winds of heaven mix forever
With a sweet emotion;
Nothing in the world is single;
All things, by a law divine,
In one another's being mingle-
Why not I with thine?

       Shelly, Love's Philosophy

CHAPTER 2

GENERAL CONCEPT OF INSURANCE

In dealing with insurance, it is very necessary that a policy holder realize that insurance companies are like any other organization. Although the aim of a viable insurance company is to serve the community in which they do business, it would be sheer hypocrisy to think that insurance companies are not out to maximize their profits, though not necessarily at the expense of the policy holders, but through a sound judgment in acceptance of risks, investment strategies, and overall administrative and management of their resources. For this simple reason, "Let the buyer beware" can never be a mere overstatement.

 What, then, is insurance? "Insurance is a contract or a device for transferring risk from a person, business, or organization to an insurance company that agrees, in exchange, to pay for losses through an accumulation of premiums."

 It can be defined as "a pool of risk." Risk is the chance or uncertainty of loss. For instance, the possibility that your house might be

General Concept of Insurance

"Capital is the fruit of labor, and could never have existed if labor had not first existed."

Abraham Lincoln

burglarized, or that you might fall from a tree while climbing, represents uncertainty of loss. From these definitions, it is imperative to note that risk is not the loss itself, but the uncertainty of the loss.

We spend our whole lives coping with risk like crossing the street, swimming, or traveling by plane. These risks sometimes result in small losses, such as loss of a key chain, pen, or pencil that we accept as a normal part of life. Unfortunately, risks sometimes result in serious financial losses, such as when a house burns down or a person is injured in a car accident. The consequences of such serious financial losses can be quite severe and far-reaching. For example, the small town of Olokoro has 200 homes worth $40,000 each. Usually, one house in Olokoro burns to the ground each year. If the home owner has to pay for the house, he or she will suffer a $40,000 loss. However, if that loss were divided among the residents of Olokoro, it would be only $200.00 a year per person ($40,000 divided by 200 homeowners). Wouldn't you agree to pay $200 a year, knowing that if your house gets burned to the ground, you would receive $40,000? Lest you forget, this is less than 0.55 cents a day ($200 divided by 365 days). "Pay little today to avoid paying big tomorrow." That's the whole concept of protection through insurance.

Now that we know the importance of insurance and that insurance companies make money by purchasing risks, it is pertinent to understand that all risk is not profitable to the insurance company and sometimes not even insurable or acceptable. Certain criteria must be met before an insurance company will accept any risk.

First, there must be a large number to be insured. The Law of Large Numbers states that the more examples used to develop any statistic, the more reliable the statistics will be. For example, a statistic indicates that one out of ten automobiles has defective tires. To confirm this, an independent research firm checked three thousand cars in 15 states.

"What is beautiful is good and who is good will soon also be beautiful."

Sappho

From our earlier example, no insurance company would like to insure just two houses in Olokoro because the two houses will not be able to generate enough premiums to cover any loss. Similarly, there would not be enough examples to develop a reliable statistic that would enable the company to assign values or premiums to these two houses. It is a matter of common sense that the company would like to insure 10,000 houses at $200 per house ($2,000,000) rather than 2 houses at even $400 per house ($800).

Secondly, the risk of loss must be definite as to the time and place that it would be very difficult to counterfeit or falsify. Death is probably the best example of definite loss.

Thirdly, the risk must be unexpected. If the result is expected, it does not qualify as a risk. The risk of a car accident could be insured, while the risk that your college suitcase will eventually wear out is not really a risk . Therefore, it is not insurable or profitable to the insurance company.

Fourthly, the loss must be calculable. Only risks for which the cost of loss is calculable may be insured. Risks which involved loss which cannot be assigned a financial value are uninsurable.

Lastly, but not least, the loss must not happen to a large number of insured at the same time. Although insurance companies would like to insure a large number of homes or people, it would be catastrophic for the insurance company if a great number of those insured were to suffer a loss at the same time. To avoid this trap zone, insurance companies rely on a principle known as "Spread of Risk." The greater the spread of risk, the less likely that there will be a catastrophic loss for the insurance company. So instead of insuring the 10,000 homes in one town, a company will want to insure these homes in many towns. This explains why an insurance company might increase your premiums even when everything is going fine with you and your company.

"To make us love our country, our country ought to be lovely."
                                                Edmund Burke

They simply have reached their saturation point in your area. Instead of refusing to insure you, they might simply increase your premium to discourage you from patronizing them. For instance, during the Hurricane Hugo in Florida, or the San Francisco earthquake, many insurance companies that have a large market share in these areas suffered a catastrophic loss. A wise insurance company, after realizing that they have insured a large number of people in one particular area, would preferably increase their rates so that they don't capture a very large market in one particular area. This is called "the spread of risks."

What if a company is caught in this trap zone and suffers a huge financial loss in one particular area, for example, Florida? What can they do? The company might increase premiums to people living in Texas to help pay for these losses. The premium increase may be very insignificant, for instance, ($1.50 X 900,000 policy holders = $1,350,000). You can see why insurance is a game of large numbers.

INSURANCE AS A CONTRACT

From our earlier definition of insurance, it is very important to note that insurance is a transaction between two parties, the insurer and the insured. When two parties are involved in any transaction, there is normally a contract. When there is a contract, each party has duties or is refrained from acting or doing something. For this reason, when a policy holder signs an application for insurance, he or she is entering into a legally binding contract.

What is a contract? To the English lawyers and to every other person groomed in the ramification of English law, a contract is a legally binding agreement between two competent parties, one party promising a certain performance in exchange for a certain consideration. From this definition we can see that not all contracts are legally binding agreements. For a contract to be legally binding,

"Teaching kids to count is fine, but teaching them what counts is best."

Bob Talbert

certain criteria has to be met:

1. Competent Parties: A contract must be between people who are competent under the law. A minor or legally incompetent person cannot, within certain legal formalities, enter a binding contract.
2. Legal Purpose: Illegal or contract against the public good, such as a contract to purchase stolen properties, cannot be classified as a legally binding contract.
3. Offer and Acceptance: This is perhaps the most important. The person desiring the insurance makes the offer by applying for the insurance; the insurance company accepts by agreeing to provide the service.
4. Consideration: This is the thing of value exchanged for the performance promised in the contract. In insurance, the consideration is the money or the premiums. The policyholder promises to pay the insurance company in exchange for the insurance. "Money talks; mine has also legs, it really walks. I sometimes wonder where it went."–Pat Umeh

In addition to the general contract provisions already mentioned earlier, insurance contracts have certain elements that separate them from other contracts. No wonder some people say, "It is very confusing."

Insurance contracts are aleatory. This means that equal value is not given by both parties in the contract. The policy holder pays a premium for which, if no loss occurs, the policy holder will receive nothing. However, if a loss does occur, the policy holder may receive a great deal more from the insurance company than the amount of premiums paid. For instance, in January 1995, Mr. Uko insured his house for $100,000 on a full replacement cost. He made two monthly payments of $50.00 for February and March 1995. By

"Success is getting what you want. Happiness is liking what you get."

H. Jackson Brown

---

the end of March of that year, a high wind blew down his house and totally damaged it. His insurance company will pay $100,000. On the other hand, if he pays his premium for 30 years and nothing happens to his house for those years, he will receive absolutely nothing from his insurance company.

Insurance contracts are contracts of ADHESION: This means to a certain degree, "One sided contract." The provisions of the contract are prepared by one party, the insurance company. The other party, the policy holder, does not take part in the preparation of the contract. Therefore, when there is any ambiguity in the policy wording resulting in a court action, the courts generally rule in favor of the policy holder. It is not surprising that some smart lawyers have made it a common practice to take insurance companies to court. Insurance companies prepared the contracts and the policy holders are jut adhering to the contract provisions.

"Beauty is truth, truth is beauty–that is all you know on earth, and all you need to know."

Keats, Ode on a Grecian Urn

EXAMINING THE FOUR SIDES OF YOUR POLICY OR CONTRACT

We have been discussing that insurance is a contract between an insurance company and a policy holder. Because of the legal or emotional consequences one might suffer if there is a breach of contract, it is very important that policy holders examine their contracts or policies and bring to the attention of the insurer any ambiguity discovered in the policy wordings. This is particularly important because each policy has certain time frames by which it can be canceled without any penalty. This is called "right to cancel provision." It normally reads: "You have a right to cancel this policy. Read it carefully. If you do not want this policy, you may deliver or mail it to the person who sold it to you or to any of our offices including our Home Office. You must do this by the twentieth day after you receive this policy. All payments made for this policy will be returned to you within twenty days after notice of cancellation and returned policy is received at the Home Office." This right is prevalent to most of life policies.

Generally speaking, each policy contract has four sides or parts. It is important that you examine these parts or sides, one side at a time. For illustrative purposes, I will call this four-sided object a DICE......

Declaration Page
Insuring Agreement
Conditions
Exclusions

"This world is a comedy to those that think; a tragedy to those that feel." -

(Horace Waldole, Letter to Sir Horace Mann)

DECLARATION PAGE

This is always the first page of your policy. It contains such information as the name of the insured, the address, the amount of coverage, the description of the coverage, and how much it will cost. It does not give details about the policy. It is simply your "policy at a glance." Unfortunately, this is the only part most policy holders read.

INSURING AGREEMENT

The next side of our DICE is called INSURING AGREEMENT.

This is the heart of your policy. It states, generally, what is to be covered—in other words, the losses for which the insured will be indemnified. This part sounds like the "Pledge of Alliance." Example: The company will pay the amount of life insurance provided by this policy to the named beneficiary or to the estate of the insured, named in the policy. The company will settle claims for which our insured is legally responsible.

The words legally responsible simply mean that not all the accidents to which the insured reported are coverable. Example: "We", "Us" referred to as company providing the insurance will settle or defend as we consider appropriate any claim or suit to which the insured is involved resulting in a coverable automobile accident.

Our duty to settle or defend ends when our limit of liability for this coverage has been exhausted.

"It is not the size of the dog in the fight, but the size of the fight in the dog."

Coach Bear Bryant

In medical insurance, the music sounds even clearer. For example:

"After $250 deductible, the company will pay 80%

(80/20) of the first $5,000 of Eligible Expenses then

100% of the Eligible Expenses thereafter, for up to a

life time maximum of $2,000,000 within usual customary and reasonable (UCR)."

What does this mean? This can be well understood by using the following illustrations:

Mr. Uche, after realizing that he was badly injured during the last summer game, purchased a medical insurance from company A–Z. He feared that he might be injured again this year. His policy has a $250 deductible, which is the part he must pay before his insurance policy starts paying (kicks in). Mr. Uche's prediction was right; he was injured during a practice, before the season began. He was hospitalized and his medical bill totaled $10,000.

USING OUR FORMULA

After $250 deductible, 80/20 to $5000 then 100% thereafter for up to $2,000,000 within Usual, Customary and Reasonable (UCR).

Declaration Page

"Do not follow where the path may lead. Go instead where there is no path and leave a trail."

Ralph Waldo Emerson

CASE

a) How much will Mr. Uche pay?

b) How much will company A-Z pay?

Answer

Uche will pay $250 deductible + 20% of the first $5,000 ($1,000 + $250) = $1,250

Uche's total payment = $1,250

This figure is called a "copayment." Now that we know how much Mr. Uche should pay, let us figure out the portion Company A-Z should pay.

Total medical bill	$10,000
Minus Uche's total payment	(1,250)
Company A-Z should pay	$ 8,750

Uche's payment plus Company A-Z's payment should equal $10,000

Uche's payment	=	1,250
Company A-Z payment	=	8,750
Total	=	$10,000

"The optimist sees the doughnut, the pessimist, the hole."
M.C.L. Wilson

Note:

Uche might not be covered for the banana he bought at the hospital to soften his voice, nor will the company pay for the newspaper he bought from the vendor to keep abreast with the companionship game. Those are not covered and do not qualify as eligible expenses.

The hospital or the doctors, on the other hand, cannot charge an excessive fee for such incident, for example $50,000. Such amount would not be usual, customary, or reasonable (UCR). It is rather unethical and outrageous.

Similarly, Mr. Uche can continue to fall and break all his legs, ankles, and hips, but once his total life time maximum payment of $2,000,000 is exhausted, he will no longer be covered by A-Z Company. Mr. Uche will simply be "on his own." He has reached his maximum lifetime payments.

CONDITIONS

Another side of this DICE is the conditions. This states the ground rules. It describes the responsibilities and obligations to both parties.

Example: When an accident occurs, notice shall be given to the company within a reasonable amount of time. If, while insured by us, you incur an eligible expense due to an accidental injury, we will reimburse the cost of those eligible expenses. The eligible expenses must be the direct result of an accidental injury which occurred while the policy is enforce.

We will pay benefits for Eligible Expenses, provided:

(a) The deductible amount is deducted from the amount payable by us, and (b) You are under the care of a qualified physician and the charges are medically necessary, and a direct result of the accidental injury, and the total amount we will pay for all accidental injuries resulting from one accident will not exceed the maximum amount

Declaration Page

"The best executive is the one who has sense enough to pick good men to do what he wants done and the self-restraint to keep from meddling with them while they do it."
                                                    Theodore Roosevelt

payable per accident as contained in our policy.

In no event shall benefits payable exceed 100% of Eligible Expenses incurred by you,

Prior authorization by us or our designated representative is required for all non-emergency care, procedures, and supplies for claims over $5,000.

We must be notified within 3 days after the date of the accidental injury in order for benefits to continue. We, referred to as company, reserve the right to review any ongoing hospitalization and/or treatment beyond 10 days in order to determine that appropriate care is being given.

Our definition of usual, customary, and reasonable charges (UCR) means the expense, but not to exceed the eightieth (80th) percentile of the prevailing physician's charges for the service or treatment as determined by one of the current prevailing Health Care charges information systems approved for use in the industry. For services or treatments provided by other than physicians, usual customary and reasonable charges means the actual expense, but not to exceed the average charge made for similar services or supplies in the locality where the service or supply is furnished, taking into consideration the nature and severity of the accidental injury suffered by you.

All this means simply that the company will pay provided you keep to your own end of the bargain.

Payment by the company is by no means unconditional, but extremely conditional.

EXCLUSIONS

The fourth side of our DICE is the EXCLUSIONS:

The exclusionary part of the policy states the losses against which the insured is not protected. Example: This policy does not apply to any act of insurrection, rebellion, revolution, or an act of war. It does not cover self-inflicted injury or injury sustained while conduction of any illegal duties such as armed robbery.

This policy doesn't cover accidental injury that occurs while you are legally intoxicated as determined by the laws of the state in which you reside; or under the influence of any alcohol, narcotic barbiturate, or hallucinatory drug, unless administered on the advice of a physician and taken in accordance with the prescribed dose.

"God gives us relatives; thank God we can choose our friends."
Addison Mizner

A Moment of Reflection
PLANNING

What is a **PLAN**?

It is a systematic action, procedure, a design to carry unto effect an idea, a project or a development.

Planning involves setting goals, developing strategies, and establishing priorities. It bridges the gap from where you are to where you want to be.

Regardless of our talent, creed, color, culture, or custom, no one person knows everything from the beginning to the end,

BUT

if you can at least know who you are, where you are going and why -

YOU ARE ON YOUR WAY TO
GREATNESS

"People don't plan to fail — they simply fail to plan."
PAT

"Religion has reduced Spain to a guitar, Italy to a hand organ and Ireland to exile."

R.G. Ingersoll

CHAPTER 3

THE MIRACLE OF LIFE INSURANCE

We have devoted the last two chapters to discourse about the general concept of insurance. In this chapter, we will be discoursing about life insurance. It is important that a reader understands the concept of life insurance because, in other types of insurance, the policy holder usually collects the benefits, but in life insurance, someone else, usually the beneficiary, collects the benefits. For this reason, it is very important that you listen carefully to this chapter.

One Mexican man once asked me, "Senor, you mean when I die, you will pay me $50,000 cash?" I replied, "No, Senor, when you die, your address will change, and I might not be able to get in touch with you; however, we will pay your wife (beneficiary) the sum of $50,000. With this money, she will be able to raise your children the way you intended. She will be able to get a new car and a new boyfriend. On every Memorial Day, they will visit your grave site and lay a flower on your cold head."

Do you understand now? "Si, Senor (Yes sir). Muchas gracias (thank you very much). I now understand what you mean." Your beneficiary will receive the sum of $50,000 dollars when you die.

"He who gains a victory over other men is strong... but he who gains a victory over himself is all powerful."

Lao Tzu

WHAT IS LIFE INSURANCE?

Life insurance is a means by which a large group of individuals can equalize the burden of loss from death by distributing funds to the beneficiary of those who die. People buy life insurance not because someone will die, but simply because someone will definitely live.

"A life insurance policy is just a time-yellowed piece of paper with columns of figures and legal phrases, until it is baptized with a widow's tears." It then becomes a modern miracle...Aladdin's Lamp. It is food, clothing, shelter, undying affection. It is the sincerest love letter ever written.

It eases the aching heart of the partner who remains behind, a comforting whisper in the dark and silent hours. It furnishes new hope, fresh courage, and strength to pick up the broken threads and carry on. It supplies the milk that quiets the crying of a hungry baby in the night. It provides a college education for the child; a chance for a career rather than the need for a job. It's a dad's blessing to his daughter on her wedding day.

Now you have known that life insurance is a miracle of paper and ink. It is important to note that this miracle will not work very well unless you buy the right kind of insurance, choose the right amount, and pay the right premium. Regardless of the situation, policy holders must try not to be "worth more dead than alive" or pay too much premium for too little insurance. Let us now examine the methods for choosing a good life insurance.

"The American people never carry an umbrella. They prepare to walk in eternal sunshine."

Alfred E. Smith

STEP I   Choosing the Right Kind

It is true that all life insurance policies agree to pay an amount of money if you die, but all policies are not the same. There are two basic kinds of life insurance.

Term Insurance

Term insurance is death protection for a certain "term", usually one year, five years, ten years, or more. Death benefits will be paid only if you die within that term period. It looks more or less like renting or leasing a piece of insurance for a few years. It generally provides the largest immediate death protection for a small amount of money. Most term life is renewable, but each time you renew the policy for a new term, your premiums will be higher; therefore, it is important that you check the premium at older ages and the length of time the policy will be continued.

Most term life insurance can be converted to a whole life. This means that before the end of the conversion period, you may trade it in for a whole life without evidence of insurability requirement.

Whole Life Insurance

Whole life insurance gives protection for as long as you live. Although you pay higher premiums for a whole life insurance than for term insurance, whole life insurance policies develop cash values, which can be used for your personal needs or used to buy additional protection. A policy with cash value may be used as a collateral for a loan.

Some whole life policies you may stop paying premiums for as little as 20 years and the policy will remain in effect for life. This is called the "vanishing premium option." While other types of whole life policies you will pay premiums to age 100 or until death

"Once there were two brothers. One ran away to the sea, the other was elected vice-president, and nothing was ever heard of either of them again."
                                                                Thomas R. Marshall

whichever comes first, no matter what an agent or a company says about their plan, most life insurance falls within those two categories. In this modern world, there is no free insurance. One way or the other, all insurance purchases lean towards term or whole.

STEP II   Choosing the Right Amount

The best way to decide how much life insurance you need is to figure out how much cash and income your dependent would need if you were to die. Can $100,000 be sufficient to cover burial expenses and mortgages? For some people, $5,000 will be enough, but some require a million. It depends on what you can afford. In any case, you usually need more life insurance when the family is young and children are in schools. Mortgages and other debts are in a high demand.

STEP III   Choosing the Right Prices

Price is the difference between what you pay and what you get back. The best way to make sure you get what you paid for is to shop around. All policies are equal, but some are more "equal than others."

You can buy insurance from an agent that works directly for one insurance company. Those agents are called "captive agents." They are very loyal to their principal (company) and often have little product portfolio.

Another better way to buy insurances is through a broker or a general agent. A general agent underwrites for many insurance companies. They are called "non-captive" or "independent agents." They have usually a larger product portfolio. With their expertise, they can shop around for you.

> *"When a man wants to murder a tiger he calls it sport; when a tiger wants to murder him he calls it ferocity."*
>
> *Bernard Shaw*

Now that you have the right kind of insurance, pay the right premiums and receive your policy in your hands. What justifies that you really know what you have?

We will examine some of the contract provisions in your policy that you should be aware of.

First, life insurance policy is a unilateral contract; in other words, it is one sided. Most contracts are bilateral. Under a life insurance contract, the policy owner has no responsibilities or obligations of any kind. The policy owner may decide to cancel or continue an existing contract at any time. The life insurance company, on the other hand, must accept premium payments and maintain the contract in force as long as the policy holder desires. Even if the insured has an incurable disease, the company must continue an existing policy in force, knowing that a death claim is imminent. The company cannot compel the policy owner to pay premiums nor can a non-payment of life insurance premium affect the policy holder's credit rating.

In summary, a life insurance contract is absolutely non-cancelable by the company except for non-payment of premiums. The policy holder can cancel at any time.

Another important provision of a life insurance contract is the "suicide clause." Even if the policyholder committed suicide, the company is generally required to pay the full amount of the policy. In most states, the only exception is when the suicide occurs within two years of the policy issue. In several states, there is no exception or only one year of leeway.

These laws vary from state to state. In any case, it is very important that you refrain from killing yourself (blowing your brains out) for at least two years of policy issue. Otherwise, you may lose both ways.

The rationale behind these provisions is that only mentally

Planning

"To love oneself is the beginning of a lifelong romance"
                                                    Oscar Wilde

insane people will kill themselves intentionally. "If a man is sick enough to kill himself within two years of entering the insurance contract, he must have been sick the day the insurance contract was signed." Hence, our definition of a valid contract is the one that exists between two competent parties. Our friend is not competent enough to enter into a binding agreement; therefore, no benefit is payable. The policy holder may have misrepresented or falsified the contract from the first day the policy was written.

Another important provision of your life policy is the "INCONTESTABILITY CLAUSE." Most contracts can be canceled if fraud or misrepresentation can be established. The life insurance contract is different in this respect. After a policy has been in force for a stated period, usually two full years from the date of issue, no claim may be denied on the basis of misrepresentation. Even if there was intent to defraud, the company must pay. The company has two years (sometimes one) to check the information given in the insurance application. Information obtained afterwards cannot be used to refuse a claim.

There is at least one fraudulent circumstance where the incontestable clause would not apply in most courts of law. If the company can prove that someone other than the insured took the medical exam with deliberate intent to defraud, the contract may be declared null and void.

Another important element is the "AGE ADJUSTMENT CLAUSE."

In the event of misstatement of age, whether intentionally or unintentionally, the face amount of the life insurance shall be adjusted to that amount which the premiums paid would have purchased at the correct age. For example, Mr. Obi, age 36, mistakenly stated that he was 32 years old when he purchased a $50,000 life insurance that costs $700.00 a year at age 32. If it was later established that he was actually 36 at the time the contract was entered, the face amount of the policy will be reduced to the amount which

> *"If you want to get rich, you son of a bitch, I will tell you what to do: Never sit down with a tear or a frown; and paddle your own canoe. So live that you can look any man in the eye and tell him to go to hell."*
>
> *Anon*

the same premium would have purchased at age 36. The same rule applies where the age is overstated. The face amount would be increased to what the policy owner was entitled to for the premium paid. Misstatement of age has nothing to do with who is right or who is wrong….It is a matter of a simple justice.

We have discussed some important provisions contained in a life insurance policy. It is pertinent to note that these benefits can be well enhanced with "extras" or optional benefits. These optional benefits carry an additional price tag or it may be automatically included and sold as a "package deal."

Now let us examine these optional benefits or what is generally known as riders.

ACCIDENTAL DEATH BENEFIT RIDER. This optional benefit rider promises to pay an additional sum of money to the beneficiary of the insured if death was as a result of an accident. The additional sum of money is generally equal to the face amount of the policy and has long been known as "double indemnity." For example, Mr. Okoro purchased a $60,000 life insurance with an accidental death benefit option. If Mr. Okoro dies as a result of an accident, his beneficiary will receive the sum of $120,000 ($60,000 natural death + 60,000 accidental death benefit option).

The premium for this optional benefit is considerably lower than separate $60,000 accident policy.

WAIVER OF PREMIUM OPTION

Under this provision, the insurance company will pay the policy premiums for as long as the insured is totally and permanently disabled. This provision prevents a valuable insurance policy from lapsing.

"Far better it is to dare mighty things, to win glorious triumphs, even though checkered by failure, than to take rank with those poor spirits who neither enjoy nor suffer much, because they live in the gray twilight that knows neither victory nor defeat."
Theodore Roosevelt

EXAMPLE

Mr. Doe, a machine operator at Toyota plant in Georgetown, Kentucky, was mistakenly picked up by a robotic computer in the assembly line. Before he knew what was happening, the robot had squeezed and smashed him several times on the ground. Luckily enough, he was rescued from the jaws of death by his fellow workers, but not until he had already broken six of his ribs, ankles, and a left hip. Those injuries left him permanently disabled for life.

Mr. Doe's private life insurance company will pay the life insurance premiums for him under this provision. This option is simply saying, "Don't worry, Mr. Doe, your waiver of premium options will make sure that your life insurance premiums are paid."

This concludes our discussion of life insurance.

In the next chapter, we will be dealing with MONEY CRUNCH — how to keep more of what you have.

"Doing easily what others find difficult is talent: doing what is impossible for talent is genius."

Amel

A Moment of Reflection
"KNOWLEDGE IS POWER"

Three men were crossing the desert by camel on a long journey. On their way, they came to a watering hole and they stopped to refresh their mounts. And as they were resting, a voice spoke to them from the heavens.

It said, "Fill your pockets with sand and tomorrow you shall both be glad and sorry."

This they did and rode on. The next morning, they awoke to find that the sand had turned to gold. As the voice had told, them they were indeed both glad and sorry. Glad they had taken some and sorry they had not taken more.

"It's no use crying over spilt milk; it only makes it salty for the cats."

Anon

CHAPTER 4

PAYMENT OF CLAIMS

Claims are made when there is a coverable loss. At this time, the water is tasted. It is sometimes used by many policy holders as a yardstick to measure the integrity of the company and their insurance policy.

This is the level that can be referred to as the "war zone." This war can be avoided if both the policy holder and the company have a good line of communication.

Many factors play an important role in a claim process. I will not devote this chapter to a major mathematical and statistical formulas used in settling claims. These are above the scope of this textbook. However, a clear understanding of depreciation will help to ease your confusion or surprises.

Do not be afraid, I will make it easy to understand.

WHAT IS DEPRECIATION?

To the accountants, depreciation is the allocation of asset cost over the periods benefited by the use of the asset. Nearly everything depreciates over time. There are many methods used to calculate depreciation. For this text, we would use the straight line method.

> *"I love to lose myself in other men's minds. When I am not walking, I am reading; I can not sit and think. Books think for me"*
>
> **Charles Lamb**

$$D = \frac{C-S}{N}$$

Depreciation = Cost–Salvage value

Number of years/ estimated life

Using the above formula, let us now illustrate.

D = depreciation   C = Cost   S = Salvage value   N = number of years

Problem 1

Mr. Adams bought a 72 inch television set five years ago for $3,000.

Following a fire which completely destroyed the television set, Mr. Adams made an inquiry and discovered that it will cost $3,000 to buy a new one in today's market.

If the television set has 10 years estimated life and $100 salvage — scrap or residual value — what is the depreciable cost in five years using our straight line method of depreciation?

SOLUTION

$$D = \frac{C-S}{N}$$

$$D = \frac{3{,}000-100}{10} = \$290$$

3,000–100 divided by 10 years (estimated life of TV set).

"Knowledge is Power"

"No man can be a patriot on an empty stomach."

W.C. Brann

1st year depreciation = $290
Therefore 5 years = $290 x 5
D = $1450

Problem 2

If Mr. Adams has used the television set for five years before it was destroyed by fire, what is the actual cash value Mr. Adams will expect to receive from his insurance company?

SOLUTION

ACV = Replace Cost–Depreciation
Actual Cash Value = $3,000–$1,450 (5 years dep)
ACV = $1,550

EXPLANATION

TV Cost $3,000
Depreciation $290 each year ($290 x 5 yrs) = ($1,450)
Mr. Adam's total payment (3,000–1,450) = $1,550

ACV means Actual Cash Value

"He that will not when he may, he shall not be when he will."
                                                                    Robert Manning

DIFFERENT DEPRECIATION LEVELS

End of Year	Accumulated Depreciation	Balance of Accumulated Depreciation	Book Value
0	0	0	$3,000
1	290	290	2,710
2	290	580	2,420
3	290	870	2,130
4	290	1,160	1,840
*5	*290	*1,450	*1,550
6	290	1,740	1,260
7	290	2,030	970
8	290	2,320	680
9	290	2,610	390
10	290	2,900	100

CASE

Now, Mr. Adams has no idea of what depreciation is. He called his insurance company and reported the incident. His insurance company said, "No problem, Mr. Adams, we will send our adjuster to your house within 48 hours."

The adjuster arrived two days later and said to Mr. Adams, "We will pay you the actual cash value for your television set."

Mr. Adams:

Actual!   Actual!!   Exact!!!

That's very good, and he reached out for a warm handshake with the adjuster.

"No man can be a patriot on an empty stomach."

W.C. Brann

1st year depreciation = $290
Therefore 5 years = $290 x 5
D = $1450

Problem 2

If Mr. Adams has used the television set for five years before it was destroyed by fire, what is the actual cash value Mr. Adams will expect to receive from his insurance company?

SOLUTION

ACV = Replace Cost–Depreciation
Actual Cash Value = $3,000–$1,450 (5 years dep)
ACV = $1,550

EXPLANATION

TV Cost $3,000
Depreciation $290 each year ($290 x 5 yrs) = ($1,450)
Mr. Adam's total payment (3,000–1,450) = $1,550

ACV means Actual Cash Value

"He that will not when he may, he shall not be when he will."
                                                           Robert Manning

DIFFERENT DEPRECIATION LEVELS

End of Year	Accumulated Depreciation	Balance of Accumulated Depreciation	Book Value
0	0	0	$3,000
1	290	290	2,710
2	290	580	2,420
3	290	870	2,130
4	290	1,160	1,840
*5	*290	*1,450	*1,550
6	290	1,740	1,260
7	290	2,030	970
8	290	2,320	680
9	290	2,610	390
10	290	2,900	100

CASE

Now, Mr. Adams has no idea of what depreciation is. He called his insurance company and reported the incident. His insurance company said, "No problem, Mr. Adams, we will send our adjuster to your house within 48 hours."

The adjuster arrived two days later and said to Mr. Adams, "We will pay you the actual cash value for your television set."

Mr. Adams:

Actual!   Actual!!   Exact!!!

That's very good, and he reached out for a warm handshake with the adjuster.

"Two men look out through the same bars. One sees the mud and one sees the stars"

F. Langbridge

Adjuster:

Pulling his pen and paper, he said "Exactly, we will pay you the actual cash value."

He immediately started writing down what he meant by Actual Cash Value.

ACV   (3,000–1,450) = $1,550
                (Cost of TV)–(depreciation)

ACV = $1,550

"Our company will send you a payment of one thousand five hundred and fifty dollars."

Mr. Adams:

"What! What! Why not reimburse me the full replacement cost?"

Adjuster:

Adjusting his neck tie and tightening his shoes should the dogs be let loose, he softly moved close to Mr. Adams, opened his adjuster's training school manual, and began to recite it secretly. "Feel, Felt, and Found." Feel! Felt!! And Found!!! Feel! Felt!! And Found!!!

With a beautiful smile, he said to Mr. Adams, "I think I know how you feel. Other people felt the same, but depreciation is subtracted because you have already had use of the property before it was destroyed. If a full amount were to be reimbursed so that you could replace it with a new one, you will be better off after the loss than before. This violates the principle of indemnity–the basis on which we and other insurance companies operate.

> *"The strongest man in the world is he who stands most alone."*
> *Ibsen*

"Although in some policies we will agree to pay you the full replacement costs with no allowance for depreciation, this can only be achieved with a special endorsement and subsequently an additional premium.

"Here is my business card. If I can be of any other help to you, please do not hesitate to contact me. We were here when you needed us, and we will be available if you should need us again."

We are the good hands people, the Rock; the Purple Shield; the Shelter; the Umbrella; the Guardians, the Golden Rule; the Pilot; the good neighbor; the physicians, the travelers, the pace setters; the Blue Cross; the Blue Shield; the Humana; the Principal edge; the Superstars; the Magic Makers; the "Shark.."

ABOVE AND BEYOND

Mr. Adams exclaimed, "Damn it! Damn it! Where is my shotgun so that I can take a crack shot on your damn head."

The adjuster fled as fast as his legs could carry him.

One thing we should learn from this lesson is that with a proper understanding and better line of communication, this war could have been avoided.

CONCLUSION

In our next chapter, we will be dealing with the Affordability Care Act, popularly known as OBAMA CARE. We will see whether the OBAMA CARE has alleviated the insurance war or whether the war has become more brutal.

"*The reason why birds can fly and we can't is simply that they have perfect faith, for to have faith is to have wings.*"

J.M. Barrie

I am thankful for all those who said no to me. It is because of them I am doing it myself.

Albert Einstein

Declaration of Independence

When in the course of human events, it becomes necessary for one people to dissolve the political bonds which have connected them with another, and to assume among the powers of earth, the separate and equal section to which the laws of nature and nature's of God entitle them, a decent respect to the opinions of mankind requires that they should declare the causes which impel them to the separation.

We hold these truths to be self-evidence, that all men are created equal that they are endowed by their creator with certain unalienable rights, that among these are life, liberty and pursuit of happiness. That to secure these rights, government are instituted among men, deriving their just powers from the consent of the governed. That whenever any form of government becomes destructive to these end, it is the right of the people to alter or to abolish it, and to institute a new government…

"An idealist is a person who helps other people to be prosperous."
Henry Ford

CHAPTER 5

OBAMA CARE

Obama care is one of the most controversial government programs ever created. This controversy stems from its likelihood of violating the core constitution of the United States while at the same time tends to be upholding the same constitution it tends to be violating. It is like a two edge sword. Most conservatives refer to it as the second worst thing to mankind since slavery.

Obama Care Compares to Apartheid

Commenting on the death of Nelson Mandela Rick Santorum, former republican Senator from PA and a one time presidential candidate has this to say:

"Nelson Mandela stood up against a great injustice and was willing to pay a huge price for that, and that is the reason he is mourned today, because of the struggle that he performed. I would make the argument that we have a great injustice going on right now in this country with an ever increasing size of the government that is taking over and controlling people's lives, and OBAMA CARE is in front and center in that."

At a closer look at Obama Care, one will not but empathize with the critic of the program. The center of that is the mandate that everyone must buy medical insurance or be penalized for failure to do so.

"Even a fool, when he holds his peace, is counted wise."
                                                Proverb XVII:28

No government can force anyone to buy anything, even if it is for their own benefits. Can the government force you to buy and eat one apple a day because it can keep the "old doctor" away? Worse still, the government is not giving the apples away for free like most other government programs. A bitter medicine to swallow!

Is Obama Care the second worst thing since slavery or the second best thing since they started slicing bread?

This can be well understood by what I call, "The kitchen table approach to Obama Care."

In this approach, you will be able to have a clear understanding of the program.

KITCHEN TABLE APPROACH TO OBAMA CARE

On June 1995, I called Mr. David Jones, age 40 white male, from our directory of small business owners operating between Kentucky and southern Indiana. Mr. Jones picked up the phone and said, "Great! My wife Debra and I have been thinking of getting some medical insurance; we are always in a constant fear of losing our roofing company we have worked so hard to build if we have a catastrophic illness. Your timing is perfect." My timing has always been perfect. We call that in the business school "target marketing."

We set the appointment at their new Albany Indiana Home at 5:30 PM the next day. I arrived a little early.

"Hello, Mr. Jones, sorry I came a little early; your home is easier to find than it appeared on our directory."

Mr. Jones replied, "Oh, yes! I know. We don't live in the Never Land," and reached out for a warm handshake.

"Come in and make yourself comfortable. You came at the right time; we were about to have dinner."

I answered, "Yep! Yep!! My timing couldn't have been more

Declaration of Independence

"The rule for my life is to make business a pleasure and pleasure my business."

Aaron Burr

perfect. Dinner sounds good. You have a nice house, Mr. and Mrs. Jones."

"Thank you," said Mr. Jones.

In sales we call this warm approach—"Breaking the Ice". In business school, we call it rapport.

As I was waiting at the kitchen table and reviewing my underwriting guidelines, Debra Jones, the wife of Mr. Jones, had finished cooking dinner.

Debra said, "You came at the right time. Will you like a plate?"

I replied, "Sure! I love chicken dinner."

After the dinner, I started underwriting their medical insurance, which comprises of many medical questions, medical kits to collect their urine, and saliva specimen.

Mrs. Debra quickly discovered that her premium is higher than that of the husband even though she is 5 years younger.

Debra asked, "Why is my premium higher than my husband's? I am 5 years younger."

I said, "That is a good question. I think I know how you feel; other people felt the same. Your premium is higher than that of your husband despite you being 5 years younger because you are a **woman**. Premiums are based on claim history and risk factors. Women are generally at high risk when it comes to medical insurance usage. They go to the hospital more than men. At your age of 35, there is another risk factor. You are still at a child bearing age. Child bearing is a good thing, thank God! In our industry, it is a risk and classified as a **sickness**.

"Legally speaking, the insurance companies discriminate against women and make them pay high premiums for being women. You can see how strong we are holding these to be self-evident that all men are created equal and endowed by their creator with certain unalienable rights to pursue equal life, liberty, and happiness."

> *"It never will rain roses. When we want to have more roses, we must plant more trees."*
>
> *George Elliot*

After the application process, and the collection of their urine and saliva specimen, I submitted all the information to the home office called the **Principal**.

Two weeks later, the home office wrote and sent a copy also to Mr. and Mrs. Jones indicating that their medical insurance was denied due to an adverse medical history and conditions found in their application.

I quickly called Mr. Jones to inform him about the bad news with an assurance that I had another option.

Mr. Jones asked. "Another option?"

"Yes, another option," I affirmed. "I told you during our last meeting that we are brokers. We underwrite for many insurance companies. I have another company in Texas; they are highly rated and stable as the company I underwrote for you and Mrs. Jones. This company has a moderate underwriting requirement, but their premiums are higher. It is our normal practice as brokers to find ways to save our clients money. We only use the high premiums companies as the last resort when the first effort must have failed. "People Helping People" on my business card is not just a slogan. It is our tradition."

"Great," said Mr. Jones. "Can you come the same time you came last time?"

"No problem, Mr. Jones. I will be at your house by 5:30 PM tomorrow to show you this second option. In sales, we call this second option a "rebound." Similar terms are used in the basketball arena after the first shot is missed."

I arrived at Mr. Jones as scheduled, and they offered me a cool aid, sensing that I was beginning to lose my (cool) over their insurance "saga."

The Jones were not very happy about the extra premium on their new insurance application. "At least we didn't have to go through that saliva and urine thing," said Debra.

> *"Winners never quit and quitters never win."*
> *Vince Lombardi*

"Exactly, that is the best way to look at it," I responded.

About a week later, the high premium company in Texas denied their application with a full return of premiums because of adverse medical history. Debra and Mr. Jones' parents died of cancer at a younger age. There is a tendency that either of the Jones will develop cancer or other adverse medical conditions that will cost lots of money to the insurance company. It is not about insuring people, but a "selection of risk."

At this time, I ran out of options for the Jones and they ran out of patience. One thing was always certain. I always remembered their courtesy, especially the chicken dinner, and they always remembered my efforts. Now you can understand that the Obama Care is not about Washington but, the Kitchen tables of the average Americans.

THE RULING OF SUPREME COURT OF THE UNITED STATES ON OBAMA CARE, JUNE 25TH 2012.

After several unsuccessful efforts to overturn Obama Care, the National Federation of Independent business, known as NFIB, took the Obama administration to the Supreme Court.

The ruling is legally knows as NFIB vs. SEBELIUS ACT. Sebelius is the secretary of health and Human Services during this period.

On the vote of 5 to 4, the supreme court of the United States narrowly agreed that Obama Care is constitutional.

Chief Justice Robert, whose vote tipped the scale in favor of Obama Care, has this to say:

"The affordable Care Act's requirement that certain individuals pay a financial penalty for not obtaining health insurance may reasonably be characterized as a tax. Because the constitution permits such a tax, it is not our role to forbid or to pass upon its wisdom or fairness." This seals the deal! Obama Care is now the "Law of the Land."

"Your present circumstances don't determine where you can go; they merely determine where you start."

Nido Qubein

What does this mean to my friends, David and Debra Jones?

The Jones can now, in the comfort of their own home, log on to www.healthcare.gov, compare plans, and purchase their desired health insurance with dignity. The same companies that rejected them many years ago are in the health care market place competing for the same business they rejected.

There will be no denial of insurance coverage based on health conditions or pre-existing conditions.

Mrs. Debra will not have to pay high premiums for being a woman. Flat rate for male and female.

No life time maximum benefits limit. In other words, their insurance will never run out.

No urine and saliva specimen or lengthy health questions. No additional premiums for adverse medical conditions.

They can't be dropped by their insurance company for being too sick or becoming too overweight.

This concludes our topic on Obama care. Now let me ask you. Is Obama Care a pain or a gain?

CHAPTER 6

Articles and References

"Silence is the element in which great things fashion themselves."
Carlyle

A Key West man who told his partner that, "If Barack Obama gets re-elected, I'm not going to be around" was found dead on Nov 8 with the words "F...Obama" scrawled on his will and two prescription bottles nearby.

Henry Hamilton, 64 year old owner of Tropical tan off Duval Street, was "very upset about the election result." His partner Michael Cosby told the police officer Anna Dykes.

Obviously, people don't really kill themselves over adverse political outcomes. But it should be said that the owners of tanning salons have unique beef with the Affordable Care Act which includes a 10 percent excise tax on indoor tanning operations as one of its revenue provisions.

Auto Fraud Wave Slams into Southland

For more than eight years on the long busy boulevards of South Central Los Angeles, drivers were recruited with promises of easy cash and a series of bogus accidents were staged. The accident "victims" were referred to a Sherman Oaks attorney who demanded hefty settlements from litigation-weary insurance companies. A chiropractor was on hand to produce phony or wildly exaggerated medical reports.

Since 1998, the scam artists allegedly staged as many as 100 collisions, winning between $10,000 and $20,000 per claim. The money rolled in.

At least it did until April 16, when state insurance investigators arrested the scheme's alleged mastermind, attorney Noel Stephen Olsham, in his Playa Del Rey home. Olsham was booked on 11 counts of insurance fraud and two counts each of tax fraud and tax evasion. Authorities also nabbed five others, including Olsham's wife and another attorney.

All told, his gang allegedly bilked insurers out of some $20

"I hated every minute of training, but I said, "Don't quit. Suffer now and live the rest of your life as a champion."
Muhammad Ali

million in phony claims. According to Deputy District Attorney David Guthman, who heads the D.A.'s Auto Insurance Fraud Division, Olsham's gang is only the tip of the iceberg.

More Fraud Cases Seen

"There will be more cases filed," Guthman promised. "We have identified over 200 attorneys in Los Angeles whose practices we believe are pervaded with auto insurance fraud cases. There is no lack of work for the people on my staff."

Guthman isn't the only one who is busy.

According to the California Department of Insurance, an estimated 10 to 20 percent of the state's auto claims arise from fraud: here in Southern California, the range is between 25 and 50 percent. The Automobile Club of Southern California estimates that auto insurance fraud costs California as much as $500 million a year — a big reason why the state's premiums are the highest in the nation.

Overall, the Department of Insurance estimates that insurance fraud — automobile and other types — costs California customers between $3 million and $5 billion each year.

Given such sums, it might not come as a surprise that California, in fact, has made considerable strides in fighting fraud in recent years.

In 1922, the state established a Fraud Assessment Commission which last year provided about $28 million to fund district attorneys' offices for their workers' compensation fraud. A 1933 law requires all workers' comp. insurers to maintain in-house and antifraud units. The Department of Insurance funds the state insurance fraud fighting activities of local D.A. offices through an annual $1 fee from auto insurance carries for every car in the state.

Poking under rocks.

"The Irish are the cry babies of the Western world. Even the mildest quip will set them off into resolutions and protests."
                                                    Heywood Broya

As a result, more fraud cases than ever are being reported to the Department of Insurance. As department spokeswoman Candysse Miller put it, "The more rocks you look under, the more bugs you find."

If California's new insurance fraud infrastructure has led to more cases being reported, it's also helping investigators catch fraudulent claims early, before large sums of money have been paid out.

"In 1922, the bleeding was horrible," said Rannie Pageler, Vice President of the fraud division at Glendale based Fremont Compensation Insurance Co. "We don't have that going on today. The money isn't slipping out the door like it used to."

Pageler said that when he joined Fremont five years ago, it was not uncommon for the company to pay as much as $40,000 in bogus claims before the fraud was discovered. Now, he says, the company is wise before it has paid even $1,000 in claims.

Of course, as companies have gotten savvier, so have the insurance scammers.

"There's a lot more of sophistication now," said Pageler, a 20-year law enforcement veteran whose fraud-busting experts have been featured on such television tabloid shows as "Hard Copy and "A Current Affair."

Zeroing in on doctors

"The managed care revolution, for example, has added a new twist to insurance fraud," Pageler said. Instead of providing unnecessary treatments, a growing number of crooked doctors are bilking companies by not providing treatment they've been paid to perform. "It's a whole new slant on the issue," Pageler said. "We have to make sure doctors aren't under-treating people."

"As a result of the stepped-up enforcement in California, many fraud mills are moving to relatively untapped areas, such as the Midwest," Pageler said. He also said that anti-fraud efforts on the

"Against a foe I can defend, but Heaven protect me from a blundering friend!"

D'Arcy W. Thompson

---

workers' comp. front are driving scammers into auto insurance and other types of fraud.

But Miller of the Department of Insurance said that, when it comes to fraud, California remains king, with as much as 20 percent of the country's total cases.

"This is a big money state," Miller said. "There's a lot of money and a lot of litigation here. We're known as the fraud capital, and it's difficult to fight that."

"A bitter pill for the H.M.O'sis to swallow hard and cut your costs," customers say.
(Administrative costs and executive salaries under investigation) by Milt Freudednheim il 33 col in. v144. The New York Times, April 28, '95 PCI (N) PD2 (L) COL 2

When 'amazing' is no longer enough, insurers raise burden of proof (insurance industry's resistance to providing reimbursement to innovative medical devices that help relieve special health problems) by Barnaby J. Teser. The New York Times, April 6, '95.

HMO bandwagon rolls on, but not all are on board. (Health Maintenance Organizations) (The changing health care industry) by Robert A. Rosenblatt. Los Angeles Times, Feb. 21, '95.

Federal workers can switch policies this month. Is their coverage a model for the rest of us? (health insurance; includes related article) by Spencer Rich. The Washington Post, Nov. 15, '94.

Picking the right benefits can save big bucks. (Your money matters) by Deborah Lohse. The Wall Street Journal, Nov. 11, '94.

Not what the doctor ordered (Abuse of Insurance Company Power in Texas Managed Care Plans) (Cover Story) by Mimi Swartz il v23 Texas monthly, March '95.

INSURANCE ASSOCIATIONS/ MAJOR INSURANCE COMPANIES

Afghanistan

Afghan National Insurance Co., POB 329, Afghan National Insurance Building Char-rahi Sitare Nau, Kabul Tel (93) 31643.

Albania

Instituti I Sigurimere te' Shqipieise (Insurance Institute of Albania).

Bulverardi Deshmoret e Kombit 3, Tirana; Tel (42) 26001   Fax (42) 23838 Manyine Director Qemal Disha

Algeria

Societe Nationale d'Assurances (SNA) 5 Blvd Ernesto Che' Guevara, Agiers Tel (2) 71-47-60Fax (2) 71-23-39 Director General Horii Muhammed Bouziane.

Australia

Australian Insurance Association: GPO Box 369 Canbera ACT 2601 Tel (6) 274-0777   Fax (6) 274-0666.

Austria

Verband der Versicherungsunternebrmen Ostriches (Association of Austrian Insurance Companies): 1030 Vienna 111, Schwarzenberg Pletz 7; Tel (1) 711-56-0   Fax (1) 711-56/270.

Azerbaijan

Gunay Anadolu Sigorta JV: 370148 Baku Hotel Anba. Tel (12) 98-32-09 Fax (12) 98-91-13.

"Knowledge is Power"

"We are sure to get the better of fortune if we do but grapple with her."

Seneca

Bahamas

International Bahamian Insurance Co. Peek Building, POB N-10280 New Providence   Tel 322-2504.

Bahrain

Bahrain Insurance Company BSC (BIC) POB 843 Smith 310 Sh Mubarak Bldg. Government Ave. Manama. Tel 255041 Fax 242389.

Bangladesh

Sadharan Bima Corporation: 33 Dilkusha   c/a Dhaka 1000 Tel (2) 252026.

Barbados

Insurance Corporations of Barbados. Roebuck St. Bridgetown. Tel 427-5590 Fax 426-3393.

Belarus

Belgosstrakh (State Insurance Company): 220029 Minsk, Kalektarnaya 10, Tel (0172) 20-62-97.

Belgium

Federation des producteurs d'assurance ie Bezique (FEPNABEL): 40 ave Albert-Elisabeth, 1200 Brussels: Tel 02 733-35-22   Fax (2) 735-4458.

"No man is free who is not master of himself."

Epictetus

Benin

Societe Nationale d'Assurances et de Reassurance (SONAR): Lot 11, US

Cocotiers BP 2030 Cotonou; Tel 30-16-49   Fax 30-09-84.

Bhuta

Royal Insurance Corporation of Bhutan: POB 77 Phuntsholing; Tel 2453 Fax 2640 Chairnam: LYON PO TSHONING.

Bolivia

Superintendecie Nacionae de Leguros y Reaseguros: Edif. Maria Cristina, Plaza Espapa Esq. Gregorio Reynolds 612 Casilla 6118 La Paz; Tel (2) 37-4137   Fax (2) 39-1819.

Botswana

Botswana Co-operative Insurance Co Ltd. POB 199, Gabarone Tel 313654   Fax 313654.

Brazil

Superintendencia de Segurus Privados (SUSEP) Rua Buenis Aires 256, 4 andar,
20061-000, Rio de Janeiro RJ; (21) 297-4415   Fax (21) 221-6664.

"All habits gather, by unseen degrees, as brooks make rivers, rivers run to seas."

Dryden

Brunei

The Asia Insurance Co. Ltd. 04!, 1st Floor, Bangunan Cadong Properties, Jalan Gadong Sera Begawa. Tel (2) 243663 Fax (2) 243664.

Bulgaria

87-69-82.

Burkina Faso

Societe' Nationale d'Assurances et de Reassurances (SONAR): 01 BOX 406 Quagadougou 01. Tel 30-62-4. Director, Gerald G Mantoux.

Burundi

Societe' National de Burundi (SOCABU): 14-18 rue de l'Amitie' B P 2440 Bujumbura. Tel (2) 26520 Fax (2) 26803 Chairman. Egide Ndahibeshe

Cameroon

Societe' Nouvelle d'Assurances du Cameroon (SNAC): rue Manga Bell, BP 105, Douala: Tel 42-92-03   Director General Jean Chebaut.

Canada

Canadian Life and Health Insurance Association. 1 Queen Street East, Suite 1700, Toronto, ON M56C2X9. Tel (416) 772-2221   Fax (416) 777-1895   President, Mark Daniels.

"No men is hurt but by himself."

Diogenes

Insurance Institute of Canada: 18 King Street East, 6th Floor, Toronto ON M56164   Tel (416) 362-8586   Fax (416) 362-1126.

Cape Verde

Companhia Caboverdiana de Seguros (Impar): Avda Amilces Cabral CP 469, Praia Santiago. Tel 61-14-05 Fax 61-37-65 President, Dr. Corismo Fortes.

Central African Republic

Angence Centrafricaine d'Assurances (ACA) BP 512, Bangui. Tel 61-06-23   Fax 61-28-24   Director, Mme. R. Cerbelland.

Chad

Assurcurs Conseils Tchediens Faugere et Jutheau et cie: BP 139 N'Djamena. Tel 51-21-15 Telex 5235. Director, Philippe Gardte.

Chile

Superintendencia de Valores y Seguros. Teatinos 120, 6 Santiago. Tel (2) 696-2194.   Superintendente, Daniel Yarun Elsaca.

China

China Insurance Company LTD. 22X' Jiao Min Xiang POB 20 Beijing. Tel (1) 654231 Fax (1) 6011869. Manager, Song Guo Hua.

"I have to live with myself, and so I want to be fit for myself to know; I want to be able as days go by, always look straight in the eye."

Edfar A. Guest

Columbia

Union de Aseguradores Colombianos-Fasecolda: Carrera 7A, No 2 6-20, 11 Y 12, APDO Ae'ieo 5233, Santa Fe de Bogota', DC. Tel (1) 287-6611 Fax (1) 287-5764.   President, Dr. William R. Fadul Vergara.

Congo

Assurances et Reassurances du Congo (ARC) Ave Amilcar Cabral. BP 977 Brazzaville. Tel 83-01-71.

Costa Rica

Institute National de Seguros. Calles 9 y 9B, Avde 7, Apdo 10.061, 1000 San Jose'. Tel 223-5800   Fax 222-2310.

Cote D'ivoire (Ivory Coast)

Union Africaine Vie: Ave Houdaliile, 01 BP 2016, Abidjan 01. Tel 22-25-15 Fax 22-37-60 Director, Jean-Kacou Diagou.

Cuba

Empresa de Seguro Estatel National (ESEN). Obispo NO 211 3, Apdo 109, 10100 Havanna. Tel (7) 60-4111. Director, Pedro Alvarez.

Cyprus

Office of the Superintendent of Insurance, Treasure Department, Ministry of Finance, Nicosia. Tel (2) 303256   Fax (2) 302928.

> *"Every noble work is at first impossible."*
>
> *Carlyle*

Czech Republic

Leska pojist'ovna as (Czech Insurance and Reinsurance Corporation) Spalena 16, 11400 Prague 1. Tel (2) 2409211 Fax (2) 24220645.

Denmark

Assurancdor Societies (Association of Danish Insurance Companies): Amaliegade 10, 1256 Copenhagen K   Tel 33-1'3-75-55   Fax 33-11-23.

Danish

Tryggingarsambendid Foroyar: Kongabruguin POB 329, 110 Torsharn. Tel 14590   Fax 15590.

Dominican Republic

Superintendencia de Seguros. Secretaria de Estado de Finances. Avda Mexico, esq. Leopoldo Navarro, Santo Domingo DN. Tel 688-1245.

Ecuador

Insituo Ecuotoriano de Seguridad Social Avda 10 de Agosto y Bogota' Apdo 2640 Quito. Tel (2) 547-400   Fax (2) 504-572.

Egypt

National Insurance Company of Egypt, SAE: POB 390 9 Sharia Sherif Pasha, Alexandria.

"Knowledge is Power"

"I have several agents working under my agency. I call them friends or business associates. It will violate my basic traditional values to allow people to work for me... They simply work with me."
Pat Umeh

El Salvador

Segutos Universales, SA: Paseo Escalony 81 Avda Norte 205, Col. Escalon, San Salvador. Tel 779-3533 Fax 779-1830.

Equatorial Guinea

Caja Autonoma de Amortizacion de la Deuda Publica. (Ministry of the Economy and Finance) Malebo. Tel 31-05 Fax 32-05 Director, Patricio N Guema

Ethiopia

Ethiopian Insurance Corporation: PO Box 2545, Adds Adaba. Tel (1) 516488 Fax (1) 517499 General Manaer, Ayalew Bezabeth.

Fiji

Fiji Reinsurance Corporation Ltd. P.O. Box 12704, Sura. Tel 313471 Fax 305679 Peter Mario.

Finland

Federation of Accident Insurance Institutions. Bulevardi 28, 00120 Helsinki. Tel (90) 680401 Fax (90) 680-403489.

France

Federation Francaise de Societes d'Assurances 26 Blvd Haussman, 75311 Paris Cedex 09. Tel (1) 42-47-93-09 Fax (1) 42-47-93-11.

"The first step to knowledge is to know that we are ignorant."
Cecil

Gambia

Greater Alliance Insurance Co Ltd. 10 Nelson Mandela Street Banjul. Tel 227839   Fax 226687.

Georgia

Caucasus Insurance Co. 380086 T bilisi Vazhe Pshevela 72 Tel (8833) 30-01-56   Fax (8832) 30-46-64.

Germany

Gesamtverband de Deutschen Versicherangswirtschah ev: 53113 Bonn, Walter–Flex–Str. 3. Tel (228) 9162-0   Fax (228) 9162-200.

Ghana

Ghana Union Assurance Co Ltd. PO Box 1322, Accra. Tel (21) 664421 Fax (21) 664988.

Greece

Association of Insurance Companies: Odos Xenophontos 10, 105 57 Athens. Tel (1) 323 6733   Fax (1) 323 6563.

Grenada

Grenada Insurance and Finance Co. Ltd: Young Street, PO Box 139, St. George's.   Tel (440) 3004.

"No story is the same to us after the lapse of time; or rather we who read it are no longer the same interpreters."
George Eliot

Guatemala

Associacions Guatemalteca de Instituciones de Seguros–AGIS: Guatemala City Tel (2) 35-2021. President Enrique Nuetze.

Guinea

Union Guineenne d'Assurances et de Reassurance (UGAR) BP 179, Conakry, Tel 44-48-41 Fax 44-17-11. Director, Maurice Giboudot.

Guyana

Insurance Association of Guyaa: 54 Robb St, Bourda, POB 10741, Georgetown. Tel (2) 63514.

Haiti

Societe' de Commercialisation d'Assurance. SA (Socomas): Autoroute de Delmas, BP 636, Port-au-Prince. Tel 49-3090.

Honduras

Camara Hondurena de Aseguradores, Los Jarros, Blvd Marazan local 313 Apdo 3290 Tegucigalpa. Tel 39-0342 Fax 32-6020.

Hungary

Hungaria Biztosito Rt. (Hungaria Insurance Company) 1054 Budapest Veda u 23-25. Tel (1) 269-0033 Fax (1) 269-0679.

"He that thinks himself the wisest is generally the greatest fool."
Colton

India

General Insurance Company of India (GIC): Suraksha, 170 J Tata Rd. Churchgate, Bombay 400020. Tel (22) 2833046 Fax (22) 2874129. Managerial Director, I J. Mahesh Rao.

Indonesia

Insurance Supervising Authority of Indonesia Jalan Dr. Vahidin 1, Jackate Pugat. Tel (21) 360298.   Director, Sophar.

Iran

Bimeh Alborz (Alborz Insurance Company) P.O. Box 4489-15875 Alborz Bldging 234 Sepahboed Garani Ave Teheran. Tel (21) 893201 Fax (21) 827196.   Director, Masoum Zamiri.

Iraq

Iraqi Life Insurance Company PO Box 989 Agaba Bin Nafie Square, Khalid Bin Wileed Street Baghdad. Tel 7192184. Chairman, Abdal-Khaliq Raur.

Ireland

Irish Life Assurance Company Irish Life Centre, Lower Abbey Street Dublin   I. Tel (1) 7042000   Fax (1) 7041908.

Israel

Zion Insurance Co. Ltd. PO Box 1425 41-54 Nothschild Blvd. Telephine Aviv 61013. Chairman, A. R. Taiber.

"It is the law of eternal justice that man can not degrade women without himself falling into degradation; and he can not raise them without himself becoming better."

A. Marten

Italy

Associazione Nazionale fra le Imprese Assicuretrics (ANLA): Piazza S. Bebila 1 20122 Milan. Tel (2) 77641 Fax (2) 780870. Chairman, Dott Enrico.

Jamaica

Government Supervising Authority: Office of the Superintendent of Insurance. 51 St. Lcuia Ave., PO Box 800, Kingston 5. Tel 926-1790. Superintendent, Patrick Taylor.

Japan

The Life Insurance Association of Japan (Seimei Hoken Kyokai): Shin Kokusai Bldg. 3-4-1- Marunouchi, Chiyoda-Ku Tokyo. Tel (3) 3286-2624 Fax (3) 3286-2630. Director, Toshiyuki Mineshina.

Jordan

Jordan Insurance Co. Ltd PO Box 279, Company Bldg, 3rd Circle Jabal Amman. Tel 634161 Fax 637905. Managing Director, Khald Dunal Hassan.

Lesotho

Lesotho National Insurance Company Ltd. Private Mail Bag A65, Lesotho Insurance House Kingsway, Maseru. Tel 323032.

"Courage is not having the strength to go on. It is going on when you don't have the strength."

Theodore Roosevelt

Liberia

Insurance Company of Africa; 80 Broad Street, POB 292, Monrovia. President, Gizan H. Mariam.

Libya

Libya Insurance Company, PO Box 2438, Osama Building, Sheria Tripoli. Tel (21) 44151 Fax (22) 44178.

Kenya

Kenya National Assurance Co Ltd. Bima House, Loita St. PO Box 44372, Nairobi. Tel (2) 333100 Fax (2) 218380. CEO D. Swaminathan.

Korea

State Insurance Bureau: Central District, Pyongyang. Tel 38196.

Kuwait

Kuwait Insurance Company SAK (KIC), PO Box 769 Safat Abdullah Al Salem Street, Kuwait City. Tel 2420135. General Manager, Ali Hamad Al-Bahar.

Lebanon

Arab Insurance Co Ltd. Sal: POB 11-2172 rue de Phenice, Beirut. Tel (1) 363610 Fax (1) 365139 Chairman and General Manager, Badr S. Fahoun.

"None are more hopelessly enslaved than those who falsely believe they are free."

Goethe

Luxembourg

La Luxembourgeoise SA d'Assurances: 10 rue Aldringen, 1118 Luxembourg. Tel 47-61-1   Fax 47-61-30-0.

Madagascar

Mutuelle d'Assurances Malagasy (MAMA) 12 bis rue Rainibetsimisaraka, Ambalavao- 1 sotry BP 185 101 Antananerivo. Tel (2) 22508. President, Rakotoarivony Andriamaromanana.

Malawi

National Insurance Co Ltd; NICO House, Private Bag 30421 Capital City, Lilongive 3. Tel 783311. General Manager. F. L. MLUSU.

Malaysia

Malaysian Co-operative Insurance Society Ltd. Wisma MCIS Jalen Barat, 46200 Petsling Jaya, Selamgar. Tel (3) 755 2577   Fax (3) 757 5964.

Mexico

Association Mexicana de Instituciones de Seguros, AC: Ejercito National 904, 6, Mexico DF.

Mongolia

Mongol Daatgal (National Insurance and Reinsurance Company) 1h Toyruu 11, Nlan Bator. Tel 313025Fax 310347.

> *"There are thousands hacking at the branches of evil to one who is striking at the root."*
>
> ***Thoreau***

Morocco

Federation Marocaine des Societes d'Assurances et de Reassurances: 154 Blvd d'Anfa Casablanca. Tel (2) 391850.

Mozambique

Emprese Mocambicana de Seguros, EE (EMOSE) Avda 25 de Sentembro 1383 CP 1165 Maputo. Tel 422095. Director, Venancio Monolane.

Namibia

Namibia National Insurance Co Ltd: Balon St PO Box 23053 Windlock. Tel (61) 224539   Fax (61) 38737.

Netherlands

Verzekeringskamer (Chamber of Insurance) POB 929, 7301 BD Apeldoorn. Tel (55) 3550000   Fax (55) 355 7240.

New Zealand

Insurance Council of New Zealand: POB 474 Wellington. Tel (4) 472-5230   Fax (4) 473-3011.   CEO, David Sergeant.

Nicaragua

Institute Nicaraguense de Seguros y Reaseguros (INISER): Centro Comercial Camino de Oriente, Km 6, Carretera a Maserya, APDO 1147, Managua. Tel (2) 72-2772   Fax (2) 67-2121. President, Carlos Lacayo.

"Be wise; soar not too high to fall, but stop to rise."

Massinger

Niger

Agerle Nigerieene d'Assurances (ANA) Plale de la Mairie, B 423 Niamey.

Tel 72-20-71.   Director, Jean Lascaud.

Nigeria www.naicom.gov.ng

National Insurance Commission (NAICOM) Plot 1239 Ladoke Akintola Blvd Garki 11 P.M.B 457 Garki Abuja Nigeria.

Norges Forsikringsforband: Hansteengt 2 POB 2473 Solli 0202 OSLO.

Tel 22-04-85-00 Fax 22-43-44-56. Managing Director, Ingvar Strom.

Pakistan

Department of Insurance: Hajra Mansion, 3rd Floor, Zebunnisa Street, Sadder Karachi.   Tel (21) 513365.   Controller of Insurance, A.M. Khalfe.

Panama

Administration de Seguros, Sa: Edif. ASSA, Arda Nicenor de Obberio APDO 5371 Panama 5. Tel 69-0444.

Paraguay

Association Paraguaya de cies de Segurol: 15 de Agosto esq. tugano, Casila 1435, Asuncion. Tel (21) 44-6474   Fax (21) 44-4343 Juan Carlos

"It is easy to look down on others; to look down on ourselves is the difficulty."

Peterborough

Peru

Associacion Peruana de Empresas de Seguros (ADESEG): Arias Araguez. 146, Miraflores, APDO 1684, Lima 100. Tel (14) 442294.

Philippines

Blue Cross Insurance Inc. Philippine Bank of Communication Building 7th Floor, Ayala Ave, Makati, Manila. Tel (2) 8150836.

Poland

Panstwowy Zaklad Ubezpieczen-PZU (Polish National Insurance): 00-916 Warsaw, UL. Traugutta 5. Tel (22) 269115. Fax (22) 269743.

Portugal

Institute de Seguros de Portugal (ISP). Av de Berna 19, 1094 Lisbon Codex. Tel (1) 7938542 Fax (1) 7954191.

Romania

Asiguarae Romeneasca SA (ASIROM) 70406 Bucherest 3, Str. Smirdan 5. Tel (1) 3125020 Fax (1) 3124819.

Russia

Gosstrakh (State Insurance): Moscow, Nestrinsky per. 3, Kos. 2. Tel (095) 299-29-42 Fax (095) 200-42-02.

"Peace shines with a double luster when set in humility."

Penn

Rwanda

Societe' Nationale d'Assurances du Rwanda (SONARWAR): BP 1035. Kigali. Tel 72101   Fax 72052.

Sao Tome and Principe

Empesa National de Seguros e Resseguros ' A Compensadora: Rua Virieto Cruz CP 190, Sao Tome. Tel 22793.

Saudi Arabia

Saudi Arabian Insurance Co Ltd. PO Box 58073 Riyadh 11594. Tel (1) 479-3311   Fax (1) 4772376.

Sengal

Syndicat professionel des Agents Generaux d'Assurances du Senegal: 43 Ave Albert Sarraut BP 1766 Dakar.

Sierra Leone

Sierra Leone Insurance Co Ltd. 31 Lightfoot Boston Street, PO Box 836 Freetown.

Singapore

Singapore Insurance Brokers' Association, c/o 138 Cecil Street, Singapore 0106. Tel 222 7777   Fax 222 0022.

"The chains of habit are generally too small to be felt until they are too strong to be broken."

Johnson

Slovakia

Slovanska' Poistovna (Slovak Insurance Co): Strakove 1, 81574 Bratislava. Tel (7) 332-949   Fax (7) 331-272.

Somalia

State Insurance Company of Somalia, PO Box 992, Mogadishu.

South Africa

The South African Insurance Association. PO Box 2163, Johannesburg 2000. Tel (11) 8384881   Fax (11) 8386140.

Spain

Direccion General de Seguros. Paseo de la Costellana 44, 28046. Madrid. Tel (1) 3397110   Fax (1) 3397113.

Srilanka

Srilanka Insurance Corporation Ltd. Rakshena Mandiraya 21 Veuxhall Street PO Box 1337, Colombo 2. Tel (1) 325311.

Sudan

Sudanese Insurance and Reinsurance Co Ltd. PO Box 2332, Sharia al- Gamhouria, Nasr Sgr. Khartoum. Tel (11) 70812.

"How far that little candle throws his beams! So shines a good deed in a naughty world."

Shakespeare

Swaziland

Insurance Brokers Association of Swaziland (1 BAS) Swazi Plaza Box A32 Mbabane. Tel 42929.

Sweden

Svenka Forsakringsforeningen (Swedish Insurance Society): Slogdt 9, 11587 Stocckholm.   Tel (8) 24-2460   Fax (8) 24-13-20.

Switzerland

Schweizerischer Vericherungsverband (Swiss Insurance Association) C.F. Meyer Str. 14, 8022, Zurich. Tel (1) 2024826   Fax (1) 2026672.

Syria

Syrian General Organization for Insurance BP 2279, rue Tajheez, Damascus. Tel (11) 2218430   Fax (11) 2220494.

Tanzania

National Insurance Corporation of Tanzania Ltd. (NIC) PO Box 9264, Dar es Salaam. Tel (51) 26561.

Thailand

Thai Life Assurance Association. 36/1 So Saparnku, Thanon Phra Ram IV Bangkok 10120.   Tel (2) 287-4596   Fax (2) 679-7100.

"Love is a canvas furnished by nature and embroidered by imagination."

Voltaire

Togo

Groupement Togolais d'Assurances (G.T.A.): route d'Atakpame' Box 3298 LOME. Tel 25-60-75 Fax 25-26-78.

Trinidad

National Insurance Board: 29 Cipriani Blvd., PO Box 1195, Port of Spain. Tel 625-2171   Fax 624-0276.

Tunisia

Societe' Tunisieene de Reasurances (TUNIA-Re): Ave Muhamman V 1002 Tunis.   Tel 891-011   Fax 789-656.

Turkey

Anadalu Sigorte Tas (Anatolia Turkish Insurance Company) Rihtim Cad 57, PK 1845, 80330 Karakoy, Istanbul. Tel (212(251 6540.

Uganda

Uganda Co-operative Insurance Ltd. Plot 10, Bombo Rd. PO Box 6176, Kampala. Tel (41) 241-826   Fax (41) 258231.

Ukraine

National Joint Stuck Insurance Company. Oranta: 252021 Kier Vue. M. Hruaheveskoho 34/1. Tel (44) 293-45-16   Fax (44) 293-15-84.

"When anyone has offended me, I try to raise my soul so high that the offense can not reach it."

Descartes

United Arab Emirates

Union Insurance Company PO Box 792 Sharjah. Tel (6) 666223.

United Kingdom

Llouds of London. 1 Lime Street. London EC3M7HA. Tel (171) 623-7100   Fax (171) 626-2389.

United States of America

National Association of Life Underwriters: 1922 F. Street NW Washington DC 20006.   Tel (202) 331-6000.   Fax (202) 331-2179.

Uruguay

Real Uruguay de Seguros SA: Julio Herrera y Obese 1365 2, Montevideo. Tel (2) 925858   Fax (2) 924515.

Venezuela

Superintendencia de Seguros: Edif Venadria 1   Avda Andres Bvello, Apdo 1928, Ceraces. Tel (2) 571-5312 Fax (2) 571-4654.

Viet Nam

Vabiet (Viet Nam Insurance Company): 7 Ly Thuong Kiet, Hanoi. Tel (4) 254 9222.

"Minds are like parachutes. They only function when they are open."

Lord Thomas Dewar

Western Samoa

Western Samoa Life Assurance Corporation: POB 494, Apia. Tel 23360   Fax 23024.

Yemen

Yemen General Insurance Company (SYC) PO Box 2709 YG1 Building 25 Al Gieirs St., Sana. Tel (1) 265191   Fax (1) 263109.

Yugoslavia

Dunav Deonieko Drustve za Osiguranje. (Dunar Insurance Company): 11001 Belgrade, Mekedonska 4 O Box 624. Tel (1) 324001 Fax (11) 624652.

Ziare

Societe' Nationale d'Assurances (SONAS) 3473 Blvd du 30 juin Kinshasa- Gombe. Tel (12) 23051   Telex 21653.

Zambia

Zambia State Insurance Corporation Ltd. Premium House, Independence Ave. PO Box 30894, Lusaka (1) 218888.

Zimbabwe

Fidelity Life Assurance of Zimbabwe, 66 Julius Nyerere Way PO Box 435 Harare. Tel (4) 750927   Fax (4) 704705.

*"O, it is excellent
To have a giant's strength; but it is tyrannous
To use it like a giant."*

Shakespeare

USA

Directory of State Insurance Departments.

Alabama

Insurance Department, Consumer Service Division, 135 South Union St., O Box 30351, Montgomery AL 36130-3351. (334) 269-3550.

Alaska

Division of Insurance, 800 E. Dimond, Suite 560, Anchorage AK 99515. (907) 349-1230.

American Samoa

Insurance Department, Office of the Governor, Pago Pago, AS 96799. 011-684/663-4116. Arizona

Insurance Department, Consumer Affairs Division, 2910 N. 44th St., Phoenix AZ 85018. (602) 912-8444.

Arkansas

Insurance Department, Seniors Insurance Network, 1123 S, University Ave., Suite 400, Little Rock AR 72204. 1-800-852-5494.

"The marvel of all history is the patience with which men and women submit to burdens unnecessarily laid upon them by their governments."

William E. Borah

California

Insurance Department, Consumer Services Div., 300 S. Spring St., Los Angeles CA 90013. (213) 897-8921.

Colorado

Insurance Division, 1560 Broadway, Suite 850, Denver CO 80202. (303) 894-7499, ext. 356.

Connecticut

Insurance Department, PO Box 816, Hartford, CT 06142-0816. (203) 297-3800.

Delaware

Insurance Department, Rodney Bldg., 841 Silver Lake Blvd., Dover DE 19904. (302) 739-42510. District of Columbia Insurance Department, Consumer & Professional Services Bureau, 441 4th Street, NW, Suite 850 North Washington DC 20001. (202) 727-8000.

Florida

Department of Insurance, 200 E. Gaines Street, Tallahassee FL 32399-0300. (904) 922-3100.

Georgia

Insurance Department, 2 Martin L. King, Jr. Dr., 716 West Tower, Atlanta, GA 30334 (404) 656-2056.

"A friend is a lot of things, but a critic he isn't."

Bern Williams

Guam

Insurance Department, Department of Revenue & Taxation, 378 Chalan San Antonio, Ramunin, Guam 96911. 011(671) 477-5144.

Hawaii

Dept. of Commerce and Consumer Affairs, Insurance Divisions, PO Box 3614, Honolulu, HI 96811. (808) 586-2790.

Idaho

Insurance Department, SHIBA Program, 700 W. State St., 3rd Fl. Boise, ID 83720-0043. (208) 334-4350.

Illinois

Insurance Department, 320 W. Washington St., 4th Floor, Springfield IL 62767. (217) 782-4515.

Indiana

Insurance Department, 311 W. Washington St., Suite 300, Indianapolis IN 46204. 1-800-622-4461.

Iowa

Insurance Division, Lucas State Office Bldg. E, 12th & Grand Sts. 6th Floor, Des Moines, IA 50319. (515) 2891-5705.

"Happy the man, and happy he alone, He who can call to-day his own: He who, secure within, can say: "To-morrow do thy worst, for I have liv'd to-day."

Horace, Odes, III, 29 MA

Kansas

Insurance Department, 420 S.W. 9th Street, Topeka KS 66612, (913) 296-3071.

Kentucky

Insurance Department, 215 W. Main Street, PO Box 517, Frankfort, KY 40602, (502) 564-3630.

Louisiana

Senior Health Insurance Information Program (SHIIP) Insurance Department, PO Box 94214, Baton Rouge, LA 70804-9214.

Maine

Bureau of Insurance, Consumer Division, State House, Station 34, Augusta ME 04333, (207) 582-8707.

Maryland

Insurance Administration Complaints and Investigation Unit–Life and Health, 501 St. Paul Place, Baltimore, MD 21202-2272, (410) 333-2793.

Massachusetts

Insurance Division, Consumer Services Section, 470 Atlantic Ave., Boston, MA 02210-2223.

Michigan

Insurance Bureau, PO Box 30220, Lansing, MI 48909, (517) 373-0240 (General Assistance).

Minnesota

Insurance Department, Department of Commerce, 133 E. 7th Street, St. Paul, MN 55101-2362, (612) 296-4026.

Mississippi

Insurance Department, Consumer Assistance Division, PO Box 79, Jackson, MS 39205, (601) 359-3569.

Missouri

Department of Insurance, Consumer Services Section, PO Box 690, Jefferson City, MO 65102-0690, 1-800-726-7390.

Montana

Insurance Department, 126 N. Sanders, Mitchell Bldg., Rm. 270, PO Box 4009, Helena MT 59601, (406) 444-2040.

Nebraska

Insurance Department, Terminal Building, 941 "O" St., Suite 400, Lincoln, NE 68508, (402) 471-2201. Nevada
Department of Business & Industry, Division of Insurance, 1665 Hot Springs Rd., Ste. 152, Carson City, NV 89710, (702) 687-4270.

New Hampshire

Insurance Department, Life and Health Division, 169 Manchester St., Concord, NH 03301, (603) 271-2261.

New Jersey

Insurance Department, 20 West State Street, Roebling Building, CN 325, Trenton, NJ 08625, (609) 292-5363.

New Mexico

Insurance Department, PO Drawer 1269, Santa Fe, NM 87504-1269, (505) 827-4500.

New York

Insurance Department, 160 West Broadway, New York, NY 10013, (212) 602-0203.

North Carolina

Insurance Department, Seniors' Health Insurance Information Program (SHII), PO Box 26387, Raleigh, NC 27611, (919) 733-0111.

North Dakota

Insurance Department, Senior Health Ins. Counseling, 600 E. Boulevard, Bismarck, ND 58505-0320, 1-800-247-0560.

Ohio

Insurance Department, Consumer Services Division, 2100 Stella Court, Columbus, OH 43215-1067, 1-800-686-1526.

Oklahoma

Insurance Department, PO Box 53408, Oklahoma City, OK 73152-3408, (405) 521-6628.

Oregon

Dept. of Consumer & Business Services, Senior Health Insurance Benefits Assistance, 470 Labor & Industries Bldg., Salem, OR 97310, (503) 378-4484.

Pennsylvania

Insurance Department, Consumer Services Bureau, 1321 Strawberry Square, Harrisburg PA 17120, (717) 787-2317.

Puerto Rico

Office of the Commissioner of Insurance, PO Box 8330, San Juan PR 00910-8330. (809) 722-8686.

Rhode Island

Insurance Division, 233 Richmond St., Suite 233, Providence, RI 02903-4233, (401) 277-2223.

South Carolina

Department of Insurance, Consumer Services Section, PO Box 100105, Columbia, SC 29202-3105, (803) 737-6180.

South Dakota

Insurance Department, 500 E. Capitol Avenue, Pierre, SD 57501-5070, (605) 773-3563.

Tennessee

Dept. of Commerce & Insurance, Insurance Assistance Office, 4th Floor, 500 James Robertson Pkwy., Nashville TN 37243, 1-800-525-2816.

Texas

Department of Insurance, Complaints Resolution, MC 111-1A, 333 Guadalupe Street, PO Box 14901, Austin, TX 78714-9091.

Utah

Insurance Department, Consumer Services, 3110 State Office Bldg., Salt Lake City, UT 84114-6901,   1-800-429-3805.

Vermont

Dept. of Banking & Insurance, Consumer Complaint Division, 89 Main Street, Drawer 20, Montpelier VT 05620-3101,   (802) 828-3302.

Virginia

Bureau of Insurance, Consumer Services Division, 1300 E. Main. Street, PO Box 1157, Richmond, VA 23209,   1-800-552-7945.

Virgin Islands

Insurance Department, Kongens Gade No. 18, St. Thomas, VI 00802, (809) 774-2991.

Washington

Insurance Department, 4224 6th Avenue., SE, Bldg. 4, PO Box 40256, Lacey, WA 98504-0256,   1-800-562-6900.

West Virginia

Insurance Department, Consumer Service Division, 2019 Washington St., E, PO Box 50540, Charleston, WV 25305-0540, (304) 558-3386.

Wisconsin

Insurance Department, Complaints Department, PO Box 7873, Madison, WI 53707, 1-800-236-8517.

Wyoming

Insurance Department, Herschler Building, 122 W. 25th Street, Cheyenne, WY 82002, 1-800-438-5768.

Thompson Drury
INCORPORATED

April 9, 1992

The Springs Office Building
950 Breckenridge Lane · Suite 295
Louisville, Kentucky 40207
Office 502/897-5111
Fax 502/897-5128
Toll Free 1-800/755-1618

Patrick U. Umeh
233 West Broadway, Suite 427
Louisville, KY 40202

Dear Patrick

The Individual Major Medical policy is selling in volumes better than Blue Cross and Blue Shield expected. I would like to recognize and congratulate Patrick Umeh for his outstanding sales in this market. Patrick has definitely found the niche to meet the needs of many of his clients. Keep up the great effort!

As usual, I have information to share regarding the Individual Major Medical policy:

- The Individual Major Medical Replacement Form is now available (copy attached). Supplies are in our office.

- Please submit all individual applications (group add-ons included) through our office. We track the enrollment and can answer your concerns. When sent directly to enrollment we have absolutely no control. Please advise your groups.

- Individual policies established on bankdraft payment will receive the initial billing to the insured. Subsequent payments will process by automatic withdrawal.

Effective immediately, Blue Cross and Blue Shield will only accept the new and simplified enrollment application. Please discard your old supplies and contact us for new forms.

Thank you very much for your continued support of Blue Cross and Blue Shield of Kentucky.

Sincerely,

Joni Skaggs

FYI: When calling BCBS Customer Service, please be prepared with subscriber's social security number and all pertinent data. It speeds the process. Thank you!

Managing General Agent for:

Blue Cross Blue Shield of Kentucky

About the Author

MAY, 1986

lations and keep up the good work, Tony.

Our crew is expecting more months like this one to come, so we'll see you next month in the *Rays*.

TYLER
JOE TINCHER, *Reporter*

We're having fun here in Tyler, Texas. These guys worked hard in 1985 and awards were given out while the celebration was held. We ate fish, shrimp and steak at a restaurant on Lake Palestine. The food was great, except I ate too much.

Leader's Circle plaques were given to Dennis Chitty and Colonel Mills. Colonel finished number 29 with the company in 1985, while Dennis fin-

New men for 1985-86.

On the trophy of the Positive Mental Attitude Award we put the phrase "that be betta." Translated, that phrase means "that be better". The native Nigerian who says that every time we have an idea is Patrick Umeh. Patrick has always had one of the best attitudes in the office; and that not only affects him, but every person in our office. Keep it up, Patrick.

Colonel Mills does not get older, but just gets better. He received the runner-up trophy and is consistent every year. We take him for granted too much, and I want to take this opportunity to let him know that he is a pillar of the Tyler district and we really appreciate him. Colonel finished number two with 1,393 points for the year.

We have a man who will be number one with the company in 1986. Why am I so bold to say that? He finished number one with our district last year and received a badly broken leg last summer. He was out several months and still did a fine job. Den-

1985 Award Winners.

shed at number 20. We are honored to have these two fine agents wearing the red ribbons at the Acapulco Seminar.

About the Author

Patrick Umeh was born in Lagos Nigeria, a native of Amizi Olokoro Umuahia Abia State Nigeria. He attended Olokoro High School, formally Santa Crux Secondary School, and completed his course of study in 1977.

Upon graduation, Patrick entered for his General Certificate of Education advanced level, successfully passed both exams virtually at the same time, and joined the Nigerian Airports Authority as a Senior Clerical Officer, a job he held successfully until his departure to the USA in 1982.

While in the USA, Patrick attended Texas College, Tyler, Texas, and by 1985, he had successfully completed his Bachelors of Science degree in Business Administration (BSC) and joined the Southern Life and Health Insurance Company as a Senior Life Underwriter.

At Southern Life and Health Insurance Company, Patrick learned the rudiments of insurance and later received the company's highest award, Positive Mental Attitude Award (P.M.A.). As a graduate of Washington National Business School and Commonwealth Schools of Insurance, Patrick opened his own agency in 1989. His agency soared to a great height. The combined life and health premiums of his company exceeded the two district agencies he once worked for in 1985-1988.

Patrick is currently a Marketing Consultant. www.patumeh.com

Membership:

National Association of Direct Marketing Executives

Revised Edition {1999}
Copyright U.S.A Library of Congress All Rights Reserved

www.ingramcontent.com/pod-product-compliance
Ingram Content Group UK Ltd.
Pitfield, Milton Keynes, MK11 3LW, UK
UKHW022222230426